WEAVER'S KNOT

POEMS

by

Glenda Bailey-Mershon

Finishing Line Press
Georgetown, Kentucky

WEAVER'S KNOT

POEMS

Copyright © 2023 by Glenda Bailey-Mershon
ISBN 979-8-88838-282-0 First Edition
All rights reserved under International and Pan-American Copyright Conventions. No part of this book may be reproduced in any manner whatsoever without written permission from the publisher, except in the case of brief quotations embodied in critical articles and reviews.

ACKNOWLEDGMENTS

Grateful acknowledgment to the following publications in which some of the poems in this collection first appeared:

"Lesson" appeared in an earlier form in Moon Journal, Fall, 2000.
"Viney Parker's Song, " " Elizabeth's Melody," "Weaver's Knot," "Answering Spring at Red Clay," "A Flatlander's Mind Rests on Peaks, "and "High Lonesome" were published in the chapbook sa-co-ni-ge/blue smoke: Poems from the Southern Appalachians, Jane's Stories Press Foundation, 2004.
"Mountain Girls Play Jazz" and "Many Streams" appeared in Appalachian Heritage, Volume 36, No. 3, Summer 2008.
"Two Poems for the Cosmos" and "Piedmont After Botticelli, 1959" appeared in earlier versions in Lunarosity, April 2009.
"Laundry Day" appeared in Employees Only: The Work Book, Poet Plant Press, 2009.
"Back When I Was Juicy" and "Liberators in the Park" appeared in The Love Book, Poet Plant Press, January 2011.
"Red Silk Sheets" and "The Efficacy of Pears" appeared in Red Silk: A Red Tent Anthology, Woman Space, June, 2011.
"Elizabeth's Melody" also appeared in Soundings, Unitarian Universalist Church of Charlotte, February, 2017.
"Near All Saints' Eve" appeared in Wagtail: The Roma Women's Poetry Anthology, edited by Jo Clement, Butcher's Dog Publishing, United Kingdom, November, 2021.

Publisher: Leah Huete de Maines
Editor: Christen Kincaid
Cover Art: Glenda Bailey-Mershon
Author Photo: Kathe O'Donnelly
Cover Design: Elizabeth Maines McCleavy

Order online: www.finishinglinepress.com
                also available on amazon.com

Author inquiries and mail orders:
Finishing Line Press
P. O. Box 1626
Georgetown, Kentucky 40324
U. S. A.

Table of Contents

A FLATLANDER'S MIND RESTS ON PEAKS 1

VINEY PARKER'S SONG 2

IN THE PHOTOGRAPH SHE LIFTS HER HANDS 4

ELIZABETH'S MELODY 5

THE HILLS' EMBRACE 6

ANSWERING SPRING AT RED CLAY 8

A "GYPSY" (ROMA!) POET WALKS INTO A COFFEESHOP 11

MOUNTAIN GIRLS PLAY JAZZ (For Grandmother Ophelia) 13

AN INCANTATION FOR MY GRANDMOTHERS 14

WEAVER'S KNOT 15

HIGH LONESOME 17

LESSON 18

CANNIE'S LEGACY 19

BACK WHEN I WAS JUICY 20

FERTILE FIELDS 21

NEAR ALL SAINTS' EVE 22

MYSTERIES 23

TWO SHORT POEMS FOR THE COSMOS 24

COLLAPSE 25

MY FATHER'S HANDS 26

BREATHE, MAMA, BREATHE 27

GARDEN ARITHMETIC 28

LAUNDRY DAY 29

RED SILK SHEETS 30

UNORTHODOX RHYME 31

MY BEATITUDES 32

LIFE IN THE MIDDLE OF LIFE 33

BALD TIRES 34

LIBERATORS IN THE PARK 36
WINTER PRINCESS 39
MANY STREAMS... 40
VINTAGE.. 42
THE EFFICACY OF PEARS.. 43
PIEDMONT AFTER BOTTICELLI, 1959... 44
MOUNTAINS MANTLE ME.. 45

For my mountain kin and mill town friends, and for the women in my family who tied knots so fine they've held for generations.
~ G.B.M.

A FLATLANDER'S MIND RESTS ON PEAKS

I am a writer born of blue lines,
sheltered since birth by sapphire mounds.

Thirty years and a thousand miles away,
I can trace their shapes against bare wall,
feel them settling around my shoulders
like a familiar shawl, beloved cousins
whose stories shaped my tongue:
sway-spined Hogback, balsam-kneed Sassafras,
Glassy with the mica dome,
fortunate Bald.

Daydreaming, like a leaf released
over time-gentled hills,
I dangle. In my reverie

spruce, hickory, cherry, and oak
reach up to pull me back
to the land of my
grandmothers, grandfathers,

to the land of butterflies and mists,
to ancestors whose bones
crumble, unloose into loam
redolent of cedar smoke and ash.

Indigo ink spilling across a page,
in exile, I inscribe
      sparkling water walls,
              stones tumbling home.

Dust falls where dust will.
As evening steals across a ridge
help me return, spirit released by fire
smoldering home over cloud breath hills.

VINEY PARKER'S SONG

Her house stands abandoned now.
Deserted, but not forgotten. At the end of the drive,
piles of river stones show someone plans
a brace to the foundation.
Great-great-great grandchildren, generations
from those she rocked to sleep, keep her place alive.

If we turned and crossed the road, climbed the hill
on the log-strewn path, we would come to her grave.
A husband, five or six of her sixteen children,
and perhaps an old hunting dog or two
lie with her beneath the piney brush.
Rattlers guard their resting place.

She lived long in these mountains. Out on
the Silversteen road, the congregation she founded
and nursed till they sang her to sleep.
All along the cove, descendants of those she treated
with herbs and poultices live to speak her name.
Viney Parker, they say—proud to own her—lived a long life.

They nod: it was a good life as well.
Few remember much about her father. All that remains
from his house, a pile of sticks left where they fell.
Like all our forebears, he escaped something. What,
no one will say. In the mountains, neighbors forget
what doesn't bear repeating, repeat

what holds the honey to the comb.
Some people and some stories brace us
beyond their time. No one alive knew Lavinia,
but in each house along the cove they tell her tale.
How she rode a mule for miles over ridges
to nurse her neighbors, singing hymns that echoed back,

reassuring the little ones she left behind.
Surely it's enough, on a cold winter eve,
watching your own baby sleep in a moon-blanketed room,

to hum a song that passed over far ridges and came
echoing down the years. To feel around you,
breathing into the bowl of night,

folks who remember someone who birthed, and nursed,
and sang. To know a thread's unbroken, stretches
like the moon's lanyard tethered to a baby's breath,
strung along the hills to the stones at Grandma's grave.

IN THE PHOTOGRAPH SHE LIFTS HER HANDS

unpinning long hair. Chestnut,
I knew only because relatives said
her hair and my sister's were the same.

In sepia, her gesture asks to be admired.
And who could not admire
the luminous eyes of youth,
the sensuous mouth,
the heavy hair about to fall?

Yet her eyes say she is puzzled,
unfamiliar with the procedure.
Innocent as a fawn in sudden light.

What I remember is her stiff hands
spinning, yarn spilling from pointed fingers,
her sharp tongue calling down
our rising spirits.

And yet the photograph . . .
Youthful beauty surprised by life.

Grandmother?

ELIZABETH'S MELODY

Long fingers pick out the tune,
deft as a canner packing fruit.
A voice, granite rich and husky,
croons in a way that brings to mind
three centuries of buried hopes and
a pack-a-day habit.

She would have liked to see the world,
sing her songs in cafés alive
with people drinking night,
mix still water from a bay
into her long lamentations,
wake ancestors half a world away
with the sounds of
ballads stolen, then returned.

But she was held here by children
who needed a mother to buy
their clothes, their father long gone.
When you've got a hard row to hoe,
you set to it.
Then her relatives needed tending,
sacred duty in these hills. And maybe
she needed the sound of
wind moving through the pines
on the ridge behind her home.

She knows where she wants to be buried.
Right here, in this plot
overlooking the road,
where people passing by
can read her tombstone:
Elizabeth ____, Family Historian.
Singer of old songs.
Mother who never ran away
except on strings of steel.

THE HILLS' EMBRACE

Walking up the Table Rock trail,
sister in front of me, brother behind.
Mist ebbs around us. Cool air
kisses our necks. Mother says
*Quit giggling, watch where
you put your feet—snakes.*
I am eight.

Walking up the Paris Mountain trail,
oldest son in front, staff in hand,
youngest behind, holding on to Papa's thumb.
Sun has burned away the mist five feet all around.
Copperhead lazes in the creek below.
I tell my boys to give the snake some room.
I am 32.

Walking up the Gloucester Trail,
Cousin Elizabeth ahead, my only child, now, behind.
A wooden bridge echoes beneath our feet. We barely see
its planks in the mist. Elizabeth says *This is where
those two boys drowned that spring the snow thawed sudden.*
"Those boys"—great, great uncles they would be—died
a hundred years ago.
I am 42.

For the first time that day I see
the peak named after my great-great-great-great
grandfather, who came, young Quaker, to this valley.
I know there is another name for here, one given long ago
by those who had nothing but reverence for this place.
Quaker and Cherokee united, flowed with Roma
and Catawba into my blood, the blood of my boys.

I am still finding the language for Us.
Grandfather, I lift my voice, not knowing
whether I mean the peak or the man.
I offer a clod of dust to the wind.

Ghosts swirl in the ebb of air—
wispy arms, kisses soft as breath.
They come to claim their own.

ANSWERING SPRING AT RED CLAY

Red Clay rustles through the conversation of pines.
The Council House, the sleeping cabins, the rangers' lodge,
massed wooden beams, melt downward
into rich ruby soil.

I seek solace here when the world strips me bare.
For my son it is the first time.
Avoiding the lodge, we gaze inside the cabins,
where the People watched logs split stars

their last Council night at home.
Now joggers and walkers nod good morning
at the trail head. As we set our feet on the steep path,
one woman leans toward me, whispers, as if a guide.
"This is sacred ground to the Cherokee.
They left from here to go west."

I know this woman cannot see that my skin
was born of these maples with the bark peeled back,
of the mud-glazed pebbles beside this ancient spring.
She sees only that my skin is not as dark as the outer bark,
nor tinged the color of the loam that lines the stream.
I feel my son's sidelong glance, nudge him,
brace my shoulders, climb the hill.

On the path, leaves cushion every step;
pin oak and white oak and red oak
mingle with sassafras and hickory,
branch wide, nuzzle rocks that
scrape our hands on either side.
My son whispers the name of each one,
as if searching for a key.

I can hear his struggle, but not the words
he needs to say. We are halfway up the mountain trail,
stopped for a moment to decide the way,
when he turns to speak.

I want to be a teacher, he says, to teach about this quartz,
about all of this—his glance rakes the hills and stream bed.
Around us, boulders and trees, wind and water
collide, settle, still. Your Earth stories will be a blessing
to the People, I say. The children will like them,
and love this place—the rocks, especially—as you do.
We turn to the Council House, where long ago

the People chose resistance. Later, they were penned here,
locked like cattle in corrals. My grandparents' voices rustle
beneath the open eaves; skitter like fallen leaves
through the words of Naneyhi: *Give them no more land.*

The wind affirms: *No more land.*
Blue Spring pulls me to its banks.
Descending the wooden steps the rangers built,
I stop at the bottom. Words jam like logs in my throat.
At the mouth of the spring, where limestone

casts the water sapphire, the banks are not empty.
I see the faces of the People,
worried as they rest in fragrant reeds,
dipping their hands into the water.

Kneeling to touch the stream, I watch
beads fall, shimmering,
from my hand. Ferns rustle.
The Old Ones stand sentinel among the pines.

My fingers sink slowly into the pure springwater.
I have brought you a warrior, I say.
At the water's edge, a sign says *Do not cross,*
but there are round smooth stones
that beckon me, and I have business on the other side.

Standing on the opposite bank,
we look down the long sweep of the creek,
racing clear through the mountains' core.

                    Suddenly there is a runner on the path.
At first, I see only his dark hair as he bends,
            dips his fingers into the stream,
brings them swiftly to his chest, his forehead, his lips.

He springs back to the path, passing us,
looks fully into my eyes. We nod in recognition.
Then he drifts like smoke down through the Council grounds.
My son wants to understand the gesture.

I explain: He is pledging his mind, his heart,
his words to Creator. My son looks at me
with eyes that have chosen the fight.
Like a refugee hiding from the invader's gaze,

I take the sage I have brought in my pocket
and swiftly crumble it into the eternal flame, the one
lit from the embers the People carried into exile.
The fire seems to hesitate before letting go
in a cloud that billows back to the stream.

Around us, everything lies still and soft as dreams.
Sacred smoke winds toward the parking lot.
We follow, our path open
through the whispering pines.

A "GYPSY" (ROMA!) POET WALKS INTO A COFFEESHOP

The audience gapes. What's this woman doing,
singing when she should be droning poetry?
I warble about having rhythm. No one knows
that's Manouche swing. It's what they asked
when I booked: Tell what inspires you.

Everything's a song, I say, letting loose again,
whether dirge or dance or ballad beat.
I snap fingers, swish my skirt.
The woman at the first coffeeshop table
has stopped knitting, pokes her husband
who looks up from his golf score, sees

I am about to show them how once
I skatted a whole poem because I wanted
to say, we Roma are here, most of us
are mixed, some got Africa in our bones,
Spain in our step, French lilac scent

beneath our nails and under our skin.
Farther away, the pulse of Rajasthan.
And if I really want to confound, I'll say
we married Persian tanbur and chang,
Turkish oud, Greek lyres and Parisian

accordions, then swung it all on a reed
with dancing keys, but I know
I only need say Django, and they will sit up.
Guitars are what Americans fancy. Now
I have to bring them down to hear enjambed

lines, marching stanzas. Somehow they get it,
smile, clap their hands to the rhythm when asked.
Yet when I finish and take my turn for the proffered
drink at the bar, people stare and point their chins,
say "Gypsy." That's all they need to know.

I sashay my way out of the shop, smile.
They will be pulsing in their beds tonight.

MOUNTAIN GIRLS PLAY JAZZ
(For Grandmother Ophelia)

This little mountain girl's playin jazz!
She can't do that! She can't do that!
She, blue-eyed, with a tanny sorta skin
Now wailin Bessie, playin Lady
Wonkin Jelly with a side a Fats
Snappin eyes and fingers on the drum
She got warriors, conjurors, Oshun come
To see her play, to hear her play
To watch her lay her rhythms in a line
We all say
Skat

This little mountain girl's gone to Paris
Stepping lively down those streets all made-a stone
In Barcelona, she felt a samba kinda rhythm
Samba kinda rhythm, rattlin bones
And birds come shrillin straight way over swamps
To bring her home Oh, sway Brazil
Just a taste-a Haiti in her bumps
Steel guitar fill
Hot stars, cool breeze, spice enough
To make you sneeze
She says: Smell that juniper in the breeze!
We all skat

AN INCANTATION FOR MY GRANDMOTHERS

Corn mother
Earth heavy
Great Raw Woman
What you must have been in childbed!

Birthing with the force of two hundred hurricanes,
crouching low, arching high, pushing out
squalling life and catching it in two fiery, rough hands.
Rocking, rocking, face like the moon over ravaged land.

Each day, I see you,
rivulets of water running out of your body
across scorched fields,
over red clay front yards singing orange zinnias.

Your daughters, we are feathers
tossed by angry winds,
falling lightly
half a continent away.

Quiet strangers riding fierce city rails,
stepping unseen through snow-hushed streets,
dancing to rain drumming on roofs,
greeting the sun in glowing glass.

Watching the moon rise in canyons of steel,
we find your image in junkyard windows,
in our own eyes, mirrored
under fluorescent lights.

We quick-step down long alleys,
flame incense in silent rooms,
fathom the earth beneath asphalt and brick,
recognize its rhythms beneath the thrum of cars.

Even city towers gleam with your life.
Skyscrapers spark starlight
in the eyes of the Ancient Ones.

WEAVER'S KNOT

Our parents wove perhaps too much weft in their web.
All their lives, they rubbed each other raw as slubbed silk.

She liked to wander. He stood still in the field,
daybreak and again at sunset, listening
for what the birds could tell. She lived to visit,
to trek up and down hills, perambulate through the lives
of anyone who would share breath. He sat and waited,
drinking after shifts in quick tosses to the back of the throat,
swallowing the bitter with the solace.

Their whole life was warp and weave.
Mother twisted every story to her own ends.
Dad picked up loose threads. Toward the end,
it was he who never minded—struck senseless
by Alzheimer's—she who paid the price in service to him.
Life reversed like a weaver changing shuttles—
rough weave, then switch to satin.

Now silence looms over their graves.
My sister and I bend, fix flowers in the gravel,
flinch at the sudden crash and chatter—
finches flush, sound like woof crossing warp.
For mother, we brought geraniums,
lovage and just a touch of rue.
Dad needs no flowers. Birdsong is his praise.

My sister pats the flowers into place,
lays a hand on each stone.
We leave the cemetery together, fingers interlaced,
fixing our own thoughts. Two sisters
different as the fawn from the finch,
(one left; one tended the parents' decline)
both captured in a web our parents spun.

Pulling away, gravel catching at the wheels,
my sister blurts, head turned back toward the stones,
I wish they could have been happier.

Without thinking, I insist,
I wish we had all been happier.
For a moment, bookends turned to face each other,
We both see how it is—escape is not as simple

as saying good-bye. A lazy mockingbird
calls down, lays a silver note of
someone else's song against the evening wind.
Over the tombstones, sun and shade,
a pattern bright as birdsong
shot through with threads of regret.

HIGH LONESOME

Tell you my story? Sure. I'll tell you about
my name, how I came to be, about the secret
that everybody knew but no one would tell,
how Mama got that blue ice in her eyes.

My own eyes are hazel. That means they're grey.
Or green. Or brown. "Why they change just like the ocean,"
the stranger said, but I was payin him no mind,
like my Grandma told me to.

Outsiders, she says, talkin rubbish. But I think
she has her head stuck in the ground like that fancy bird.
She passes right by all those artsy shops on Main like it was
still Buncombe Highway out there, corn fields on both sides.

She pretends it's just us, livin here still, but really
there's more "outsiders" than us, these days.
Got to catch up to the times, I think.
But I don't say it, just keep wiping the counter and
servin up eggs and grits to men don't wash their hands.

Don't mean I got to go listenin to no sweet-talkin
flatterer. Men can hurt, but they don't often help.
Mama taught me that. Still, I'd like to see the ocean.
What if it really is the color of my eyes?
That's what I started to tell. How Mama changed my name—

Dad's not in the picture, if you get my drift.
Named me, then left—"Change your name,
change your story," Mama always says.
Everybody knew the story, anyway.
So, about the blue ice in Mama's eyes,
and how I came to be. Stop me if you've heard it before.

LESSON

Daughter, this is your womb.
She put her warm hand
on the child's belly and drew
the outline of a cave.

Out of this cavity
you will draw that which is
most precious to you.
Into this space

you will draw that which is
mysterious, unknowable.
She drew a line from
the womb to the heart.

This is the straightest of lines.
Do you understand?

CANNIE'S LEGACY

Gramma's hands, swollen at the knuckles,
nevertheless played fine with threads
of all kinds. Embroidered gifts—hand towels,
pillowcases, sheets edged lacy colors—gladly
received linen appreciations of kinship,
marriage vows, fertility, in bright blues, pinks,
yellows. In every knot keen estimation,
where to draw the line,
rolling each length to a fine point.
Where did she learn to sew so well?
Her mother? No, her mother had no time
away from four rambunctious boys.
Roosevelt, she said. The president
saved our lives when he opened sewing
halls, where we made uniforms, but also
fine goods for rich people. Her eyes gleamed,
happy to give the best to those she loved.
Now I lay myself down to sleep
on pillowcases fit for a queen, scalloped
on every edge with a hint of aquamarine.

BACK WHEN I WAS JUICY

Back when I was juicy
I pried the lid off morning,
knifed from my bed
onto cold floorboards,
scattered pennies
enough for coffee in the café,
or a luscious scrum of chocolat
on a cold Sartre afternoon.

Virgin among molded tomes,
I, willing wand of destiny,
jumped to conclusions about infinity
while frat guys in the booth behind
bet on the constants of integration.

Down the long green moments
I strode, confident, to and from
class, shouldering book bags,
tippling volumes from overhead shelves,
palming change like bribes
for fortunes, assured of redemption
in the hands of destiny.

Every Saturday, I rambled bookstore
to bookstore among other explorers,
seeking keys to unlock furtive encounters
behind mothers' cast-off lace curtains.

Jampot oozing thick syrup seeds,
I melted into one after another
armored knight. Later, we read each other
tales we could not fathom
back when I was juicy.

FERTILE FIELDS

Plowed fields anticipate rain,
open, yield moisture
staining dry furrows deeper
brown, wet along the crease.

Pressed for time, late, exhausted
by chaos of wind whirling
grit, we awake from a roadside nap
to spatter on our windshield,

stop

inhale the deluge

coming,
        coming,
                coming.
Here.

Raging storm, fecund
like arriving at the moment
the universe
unlocked for business.

Grateful for pores that can breathe
both air and rain, we remain open
all day, like a flower
stunned by its good fortune.

NEAR ALL SAINTS' EVE

Today's rain spat ice, snapped
willows, heralds of a scolding season.
Trees spill color into streets full of fright—
mischievous teens cavorting among
tattered, scared crows, hobgoblins
clinging to parents' wrists. Gold leaves

clutter gutters. We warm our bones
with hot cider, drain even dregs
of chocolate, wrestle snow tires,
send ancient mowers to rest.
Preparations swirl as the world
dies down. Ditches fill

with scattered seed. Not like we haven't
been warned. We've had weeks
to rescue late roses from first frost.
Still, we linger on wet porches,
dreaming a rarer red from maples.
Even dying has its beauties, I say

to my mums, drowning in late monsoon.
Inward, restless ghosts. The wind tosses
bones to winter, which arrives whistling
like a surprise we have coming.

MYSTERIES

Do I believe in mysteries, she wants to know—
Indigo children, sudden signs in the desert.

I consider. Maybe I carry them with me?
My grandmother resting comfortably

behind my teeth, forgotten runes slipped from
my sleeve on the evening walk.

Constellations spin while we wash the spoons.
Minerals sparkle like stars in the dishwater.

Our toes stir molecules.
So what, you say? Ephemera. Illusions.

No, I say, evidence
that we are emanating

ingesting
pulsating

to a hidden beat.
Step softly, now.

Worlds crash with your turnings.
What is the Holy Ghost

but mortality melting on your tongue?

TWO SHORT POEMS FOR THE COSMOS

1.
What are we, but cunningly organized particles
stirred by whatever tickles or disrupts?
Or strings, perhaps strings,
vibrating out into the spheres
where some force,
for want of better pastimes—yanks?

We pray, lift voices in psalms,
pulse joy, anger, quasars
speeding up to destruction,

permanent or not.
Maybe some parallel world awaits,
magnetic arm thrust out from a tear
so deep no one, no thing returns.

But what if all paths disintegrate
towards ecstasy?
Trajectories
stretching to starfields
awakening tiny Gods
bursting forth in spasms of delight?

2.
Son pours constellations of Cheerios
into his milky bowl,
spoon to mouth, black hole stirring stars.
Around his place a galactic army,
soldiers on important missions, monsters
offering heroes a chance to shine. Outside
our sun-smeared window,
sunlight striking Earth.
His face a perfect sun of innocence.
If you could choose, would you be plucked
or stirred?

COLLAPSE

CRASH! screams the Emergency Room TV.
I strain toward the screen, can't make it
come out any differently—
Rain-slick road, eternity
between lights, late hour carelessness,
two mothers, three children
dead on the scene. Blink, and they
are hurtling into these hospital

corridors on gurneys. One dad arrives
face crumpling as he claims membership
in our lonely club—Parents outliving children—
I know that nothing I can say will dim his sensation
of speeding through a universe of inexorable collisions
but I go to him, anyway. We collapse inward
even as we impel ourselves
into each other's arms.

No wall more solid,
no atom less wanted
than grief. His face is a moon of anguish
overtaking my starry sky.

MY FATHER'S HANDS

My father's fingers curved, grasping, empty,
except for a lit cigarette, cupped
inward, as if to consider self-injury.
Tales from the library about far-off places,
men who spoke their piece with ease,
dangled, teasing, in front of his nose,
while he went off to work
each night in the clamoring mill.
He stank of liquor, sweat, disappointment.

What I remember most about my father
is the scratch of calluses on my skin
and the dampness of despair in the room.

That, and when I was eight, wearing glasses
for the first time, watching leaves cast perfect
heart-shaped patterns on the sidewalk,
how he taught me to skip, holding my unbroken skin
in his rough paw as we bounded
without a care down the pocked and pitted pavement.

How some days the ground settles
beneath your feet, and you push forward
without tripping once.

BREATHE, MAMA, BREATHE

Mama, let go my hand. Nurse says you've had a stroke.
I have to call Brother. Sister, shake her. Remind her
to fill her lungs. In. Out. *Breathe, Mama, breathe.*

Outside, rending wind and rain. Remember, Mama?
The hurricane, palm trees thrashing ground, your hands
steady on the wheel? I was six. *Mama, don't let go.*

Your temperature rises as you struggle for more time.
Breathe in. Again. Again. Pinch your good hand,
rub the blue one. Whispering: *Breathe, Mama, breathe.*

The room fills. I step aside, waiting against the wall.
Time slips. I am two, wailing as you grasp my arm, break
my heart the first time. *No! I didn't do it! Mama—let go.*

Was I two? I am two hundred now. My reluctant hand
against your burning cheek, heart strung between groans.
Another voice says, *Breathe, Mama, breathe.*

The brother, aunts, come, go. I count birthdays, holidays,
rewind strings of memory. Your pulse is slow.
I pray for that next gust. *Try to breathe, Mama, breathe.*
One soft breath, held forever. Kiss your face. Say *Mama.* Let go.

GARDEN ARITHMETIC

In the garden square, planeloads of asters
transect late lilies. The requisite cat

appears, whiskery fog of grey fur
in stonewashed, milky sun.

Butterfly plus bee equals milkweed pods,
infinite vibrations. Wisteria-draped bench,

soft-edged shadows, hymns of roses
celebrate order among the roots.

Where are woes today? Our wounds?
A balm for all thrives here

beneath the round-leaved plum,
sorrow swept clear by willow fans.

Honey accrues in reeds, pools,
hours creep, frogs leap round the 'dial;

starlight in abundance falls to Earth.
Watching the descent, I bend

to account and find the sum of tears
is solace here.

LAUNDRY DAY

Rain has taken Earth
by its corners
and given it a shake,
whisking away
dirt and grime.

Clouds hang
fluffy as a baby's sheet
sailing, though anchored
between the poles of trees.

Awakened by a sudden trill of birdsong,
we hang our sorrows out to dry.
When we take them in again
they will smell
like air and sunshine.
We will know them only
by their sharp beaks.

RED SILK SHEETS

Mama has gone and left me
her place at the table. Such
high expectations: Crones
comfort the sick, amuse the young
with stories one is tired of telling.
Anyway, children never get the point
till their goose is cooked.

And so much one cannot do—
squander money; forget
to put out the cat; dance dirty
at weddings—lest the kids
bring up nursing homes.

Time was, the only choice was to master
that Everyone-else-here-is-wet-behind-the-
ears-voice. And fake deafness so you
could give the whole room the benefit
of your opinion, with no interruptions.

I'll break new ground. Here on,
no suffering fools or ignoring
contradictions. Next week
I'll buy red silk sheets. Let them
flap on the line for everyone to see:
an unfettered woman lives here.

UNORTHODOX RHYME

Preachers tease us with heaven's riches
Make us choose—wives or whores
Warn us, we're too big for our britches
Then forbid abortion, divorce

Warn us we're too big for our britches
Want us to scratch all their itches
Then forbid abortion, divorce
Good men writhe with remorse

Want us to scratch all their itches
Scratch our own, they call us witches
Good men writhe with remorse
Veils conceal life's source

Scratch our own, they call us witches
Force us to choose—wives or whores
Veils conceal life's source
Camels pass by your riches.

MY BEATITUDES

Thanks to the universe for joyous ones
who wear earrings that jangle
and rings on their toes.

Blessed are our fruitcakes
who tease us with the latest slang
so that we forget their many talents—

how they sing our morning coffee,
how they dance across our desktops
trailing hearty laughter,

how they skip across each field of play.
(They invented playgrounds, jungle gyms
and rope walks and all the jump rope songs,

flip-flops with colorful daisies between our toes,
every blooming idea.)
They invite us out for margaritas,

convince us to stay up too late
dancing to the loudest bands.
They never fail to see the stars.

Every cherished misspent hour
happens because someone forgot to grow up,
simply refused to forget the punch line

or keep the dog on leash.
Blessed are the rule-breakers,
for they need to inherit nothing.

LIFE IN THE MIDDLE OF LIFE

Girls on a tear
swapping cheerleader yells
as they twist down the street
wrapping each other's braids
on a timeless moonlit night,
belly up under the sun taking care
to match their tans, riding bikes
against the wind, strong calves pumping

Old women in a spin
failing to take out the trash
till the day after rancid,
writing checks, putting them
in wrong envelopes, taking ancient aunts
out for tea, their grandchildren
out for a movie, their best friend
to the hospital for chemotherapy

Old writers leaving home
with nine dollars in their pockets
and verses in their ears
serving wine to mere strangers
in the veranda at noon, making time for
birdsong in the midst of brutal days,
pounding sense into the world
one line at a time
making love to the whole universe
in one long sestina

Three people on a deserted beach at dawn....

                And one dog sails away.

BALD TIRES

Fearless young, we slid on boxes
downhill, nicking railroad tracks,
tumbling onto highways, scaring
wits out of drivers who wagged
fingers and heads, warning
while we scrambled up the hill

for another go. Toenails
ripped out at the roots, bloody shoes,
small price for that delicious
lurch of terror in our throats.
Best were the days when we left
school, raced the 2:15 to

the bottom of the hill, made
the engineer, mad as hell,
blow his whistle, braking
with all his might. The closer
the race, the bigger the smiles
when we leant our boxes in the shed.

We smirked like dizzy chipmunks
at grownups' warnings. Claimed it
was all an accident. Hadn't meant
to go that far. Now I blow
into my steaming cup at
the garage just off the square

while Brother buys whitewall tires.
Watch the kid with stewed-prune eyes
wait, twitching, while his ride gets
its threadbare rims pumped up.
My teacher's eyes tell me he's
using, sure, but what? I toss

my cup, shrug—limited by
a different set of dangers.
What is it like to score drugs

in a town with no back alleys
or weedy lots, just fields and
prim lawns? The kid hunches

his shoulders, blocks my prying eyes.
Watch him pull away, threadbare
Goodyears squealing. I wonder
which is crazier, driving
bald tires on two-lane curves or
shooting crack in a small town?

I imagine him crouched in
cornstalks, seeking out his own
shortcut to the stars. An urge,
call him back, point out dangers.
But who am I? A former
miscreant, he'll read it in

my eyes like I saw it in
angry faces of those who
shook their fingers at my gang.
I remember wet pavement
leaping toward my face, car lights,
engines' roar, sweet rush of fate.

I wonder if this kid feels
like he's skidding when needle
punctures vein, why we feel most
alive when we're dodging trains.
Car's ready, time to go, for
a second I gun the motor,

pretend I can't find the brakes.
It's no good. I brake, and rediscover
Old age screeches
louder than tires out of tread.
It's hesitation that lays rubber.

LIBERATORS IN THE PARK

He has seen me in the park, holding a candle
for peace, wants to give me something
for my trouble, he says, and holds out a cross of palms.
Dead fronds fall from the park's trees.

He picks them up while talking to his friends—hippies,
artists, homeless vets who haunt the square—ghosts
amid tropical foliage, and the runaways, on the fringe.
Nowhere to go till the shelter opens.

He makes crosses 'cause he's on the right path now.
He wants to tell me his story—he's going to tell me
as I wait, mind jangling errands and chores,
not looking at the cross—not my religion, anyway.

I'm a drunk, he says, but I got a job, night manager
down at the shelter. *Can't drink no more,
takin' care of my buddies* now. I been in war. . . .
He stops, twists the long leaves, which bend,

jungle grass in his hand. A scrim of hair
around his pink scalp, must be fifty or sixty.
Da Nang, Khe Sanh, or somewhere else
halfway around the world. He looks down,

twists some more, starts again: *I'm a drunk, but—
Me and my buddies, we're broken but we're brave.
We come out here each night, the tourists stare,
the cops try to move us on. Hell, we got nowhere to go,*

but we're tryin to get there. . . . He's missing a synapse
or two. I don't want to cut him cold in front of my son,
so I say Why not the VA counselor over on One?
He nods vigorously. *Yeah, he's a good man, but he don't got*

what we need, tries to send us to rehab over in Gainesville—
Hell, ain't none of us got the bus fare home. 'Sides I got friends
hooked on the drugs the VA give 'em. Why can't they give us
a job, a little cash, a place to come home to. Hell, don't nobody

care, vet or not. But you and your friends, you come out here—
I eye his friends, a ragtag knot, hands in their pockets,
devils in their eyes, clumped together. One stabs a cigarette
into the base of a potted plant. They can't tell how much

I want to get away, to get rid of this stupid cross,
explain about patriarchal symbols, about being Unitarian,
how God the Father isn't part of my Universalist dogma.
But the night manager is sweating. There's no logic

to what he's telling me: he fought for America,
but America don't care. *Still you gotta stay on the right path.*
I'm a drunk, but I'm not a bad man, he's saying. *I like to make*
these crosses, pass them out, if I see a person doing good—

You gotta reward kindness. And no ma'am he don't want money,
but the men at St. Francis House could sure use a hand.
People like me know that, but the government sure don't.
Why don't they just find us jobs? His high-pitched whine

is getting to me. *I dunno, but you send kids over to kill*
and die . . . maybe you should fix them up when they
come home broken. We don't want handouts or drugs from
the VA, what we want is . . . He stares at the Bridge of Lions

like the wind will tell him what to ask for. I shrug.
I don't know what he wants—Yes, I do, I do know.
He wants me to look him in the eye, take this cross
and say it means something to me, too, and I know

he's a drunk, but he's also kind, with a big hole in his heart.
And maybe if I slow my beat down, if I quit revving
my engine, I can find the right wavelength for us both.
And then I remember Lucretia Mott in her Quaker bonnet

saying not God but men and women make slaves,
not Christianity, but priestcraft demands women's silence.
It's not the religion but the practice that makes us lose our way.
And I remember Harriet Tubman, retiring from liberator and spy

to nurse poor black people freed from slavery into poverty,
because we all lost our religion too soon.
And I think of St. Francis, how the animals couldn't know
he was a priest, but they understood the compassion in his eyes,

like the blue orbs on this jumpy man in front of me.
So I stick out my plain Unitarian hand and I open
my strong Amazon lips and I say *Thank you, Friend.
I have a place for this at home.* And I know I will stick it

among the potatoes and the wilting onions, move it
from place to place because I don't know what to do with it.
As I walk away, I pray, Good Friend Lucretia, help me remember
the gentle speech. Mother Moses, keep my hands full with work.
And Dear St. Francis, help me to change myself, always myself, first.

WINTER PRINCESS

Snow again on Michigan Avenue, not yet on Devon.
A Roma girl departs the Slavic bakery,
pulls a thin raincoat over her pink uniform.
She carries the aroma of bread under her arm.
Sky leans close.

A sudden puff of wind forces her chin up,
to see a lost brace of Canadian geese
stitching patterns in the darkening night.
She imagines a cloak of deep, soft down
falling across her shoulders. The crowd
turns white velvet to grey slush.

The winter princess turns away.
Her slippers imprint a glittering pattern
in an alley dim as medieval moat. On Michigan,
women in thick furs pass wary nannies,
their charges bundled into chariots;
hats mimic those of other eras.

Traffic lights blink red, yellow, green.
On the corner, a man selling news of homeless people
stamps his feet to keep warm. His eyes light
on a trail of diamonds in the snow. Women's backs
everywhere he looks. How will he know?
High above them, the stars await a sign.

MANY STREAMS

1
Muddy bone rises from many streams,
storm-shaken bits come to rest
in plants and bushes,
many-petaled skeletons
ablossom beside front steps.

Up the trail mountains confuse
us with splendor, purple misted arms
enfolding, wrapping their girth across vision:
layer upon layer, green, blue, purple spectrums;
while mingling in the valley

dirt, our natural color, and universes abloom:
sky, sun, moon, stars, kaleidoscopes
surround. Ocean's thrill and pull
whispers at our backs: This is not your home.
Come with me to the hole in the mountains.

Across the sea. Back home to Africa.
Old women in shawls cover
their faces, bent, glinting
secret jewels and shells, rattling in our ears.
Children in the garden

speak in voice of Corn Woman,
discover sacred offerings crawling paths.
Mud calls our name, grabs our ankles,
pulls us into slip and slide, tumbling creeks
rising from chasms in Mother Earth.

Laurel switches sting our faces,
quartz flies against our feet
as we roll down slopes of shining rocks,
stumble against cedar,
come to rest at precipice.

All the Earth
lies at our feet, in every molecule
a wealth of worlds.

2

Always, I'd rather be traveling
amid indignities, superfluous magic,
practicing human, learning to fall,
grasping hands extended by strangers,
perfect along the way. Honey in the pot
at the next diner, mica glistening headlights,
asphalt. Horses promise they will spirit me away.

On the highway, night mist against fences,
mysterious farms. Stamens call my name.
Cabbage cries out in the night,
like a child imploring witness to growth.
Imagine sunlight, captured by cells
of ingenious design.

I will not remain, but bolt before harvest.
There is too much to hear, too many calls
overdue in the world not vertical.
I will be back to the meadow mowed at sunset,
and the moon come tipping ghostly
over the ridge. I will be back
when snows hush every stream.
To rest, rest, in the nothingness
of cellular repose.

VINTAGE

You bore the basket high on your shoulder
till we came to the wine cellar table; stood,
hands on hips, reading labels out loud
for the pleasure: cinnamon claret,
ruby cabernet, blackberry muscatel.
We picked fiery chili sauce from a mountain
of Mason jars, got drunk on fragrant stock,
pink as the cheeks of the girl who sliced cheese.
We smiled over her unimpeachable braids,
threaded through checkered tables,
slick with succulents we might sample,
and walked home through sun-drenched streets,
elbows tickling together, like avocadoes
and oranges mingling scents
at the bottom of the basket.

THE EFFICACY OF PEARS

If I have to grow old
obsessed with inner
workings,
let me wrap my fiber
in golden light,
tap out the final days
mellow to the faintest
tinge of dappled green, spots
only a painter or a mystic
wouldn't shun. Redolent,
reminiscent of fine autumn
Chardonnay. Fig fills the mouth
with seeded riches. Give me texture
that yields against tongue and teeth.

See how the pear
stands sentinel in
white blossom,
bride to morning light,
rosy fruits
opening toward night.

PIEDMONT AFTER BOTTICELLI, 1959

I have loved the taste of plums.
On a porch gazing at River Falls,
an adult reached over my history book,
handed me a purple fruit,
said, Taste, and I did.
Juice exploding my tongue
like a thousand bees
making honey just for me.
Sugared purple swirling blue peaks
sun glinting water hills
looked fondly on like all gods rolled
into one voluptuous Spirit.

I saw before me, Tuscany:
sunlit splendor, Umbria
naming colors orchard fresh,
cold marble stirred to life,
Brunelleschi's domes aglitter
among the barns,
Venus stepping from her shell
clothed in breezes soft as
rich lingering velvet, pip
pouring out slow glory
over stubbled fields.

Now, forty years on,
juiced with ginned-over
memory, I eat plums
amid Burnt Sienna
blooms, my modest hills
landscapes dipped in honey.
For a moment, on a Carolina
porch, I taste Italy,
and life resembles art.

MOUNTAINS MANTLE ME

Above the treeline, where air is thin
yet rich like honey in the lungs,
I watch stars cartwheel
through ancient dust.

Inhaling cloud's breath,
I finger rocks, bits of ancestors
buried here so long ago
they have turned from particle to crust.
I dissolve into them,
let the mountain mantle me,
feed me silt and barite,
flow its long-buried lava
through my throat.

This mountain, its fires
slaked low, will be the last of Earth's
creations to fall.
And I will fall with it,
ancient dust
        cartwheeling
into stars.

-THE END-

Glenda Bailey-Mershon has worked as a bobbin threader, a bartender, a bookstore and small press owner, and a university administrator. She has taught women's studies, anthropology, and writing in various institutions, as well as GED English preparation for Romani youth.

She co-founded and led several women's organizations in Illinois, including chairing the Illinois NOW PAC, and co-founded Women's Lobby Day with Luellen Laurenti. She worked for a while as a political operative and appears in the reference book *Feminists Who Changed America, 1963-1975*, edited by Barbara J. Love.

Her love of history and years of work in the civil rights movement, beginning as a fourteen-year-old in the Greenville County bus boycott, led her to co-direct with Barbara Vickers the Roots and Flowers Project on one of the nation's oldest Black settlements, funded by the Florida Humanities Council and in cooperation with the St. Augustine Historical Society. She also directed an oral history project on that city's civil rights movement, which culminated in the short film, *Somebody Started Singing*. She won an Award of Merit from the Illinois Historical Society for her work on the history of the 1950s-era planned community, Park Forest.

Through poetry, fiction, and nonfiction, she explores the experience of being "mixed blood" in America. Her poetry chapbook, *sa-co-ni-ge/blue smoke: Poems from the Southern Appalachians*, funded by the Florida Division of Cultural Affairs, explores the links between Cherokee and European cultures in the mountains. Her novel, *Eve's Garden* (Twisted Road), evokes the voices of a Romani grandmother, her daughter, and her granddaughter, each of whom experiences tragedy, racism, and the redemption found with friends and family. She co-founded Jane's Stories Press Foundation, which offers the Clara Johnson Award for Women's Literature and has a mission to spotlight diverse women's voices in the publishing industry.

Glenda has been a finalist in Our Stories fiction contest; featured author at Knox College, Flagler College, Trine University, and other institutions; and has read widely in bookstores, libraries, and in readers' homes, as well as over Zoom.

www.ingramcontent.com/pod-product-compliance
Lightning Source LLC
Chambersburg PA
CBHW020343170426
43200CB00006B/488